M000205538

QUIET

LIFE

THE Quiet Life

RAY ASHFORD

DIMENSIONS
FOR LIVING
NASHVILLE

THE QUIET LIFE

Copyright © Ray Ashford

First Dimensions for Living edition 1999

Library of Congress Cataloging-in-Publication Data

The quiet life / [compiled by] Ray Ashford.
     p.   cm.
   ISBN 0-687-03489-2 (pbk.)
    1. Christian life—Quotations, maxims, etc.
    2. Conduct of life—Quotations, maxims, etc.
 I. Ashford, Ray.
 BV4513.Q54   1999
 241'.4—dc21   98-44292
                                 CIP

Scripture quotations noted NRSV are from the
New Revised Standard Version Bible, copyright ©

Contents

Stillness

*L*eaving a clamorous, discordant world, I stand motionless in a clearing deep in the woods. Around me the snow is soft and deep, a dazzling white, overhead the sky a perfect, cloudless blue.

I can hear, barely, my own breathing but nothing more: no hiss of skis, no birds, no voices, no hum of distant traffic, not even the sigh of an errant breeze.

In a silence so total, so pure it is almost palpable, a thought occurs: how sad that such moments are so rare.

When from our better selves we
   have too long
Been parted by the hurrying
   world, and droop,
Sick of its business, of its
   pleasures tired,
How gracious, how benign, is
   Solitude.

—WILLIAM WORDSWORTH

We once lived beside a
four-lane highway on the out-
skirts of a large city. We bought
the place, in spite of its loca-
tion, because it seemed to be,

as the realtor put it, "a lot of house for the money."

As the city grew, however, the highway also expanded. Four lanes became eight, then twelve, with the traffic reaching enormous proportions. In the wintertime, windows were closed and there was a measure of peace. In the summertime, though, when windows were open, the roar of the traffic day and night was appalling.

Yes, we lived once beside a busy highway but never again.

———————

Muzak fills our elevators. Hard rock blares out of cars and boats

and apartment house windows.
People jog down highways with
earphones on and bicycle along
city streets balancing boom boxes
on their handlebars and sit in
airports with transistor radios
against their ears, all of them
insulated against the world
around them and, most of all,
protected against the searchings
within themselves.

—JOAN D. CHITTISTER
Wisdom Distilled from the Daily

Where shall the word be found,
where will the word

Resound? Not here, there is not enough silence.

—T. S. ELIOT
"Ash-Wednesday," in *The Complete Poems and Plays*

*S*tanding around, struggling to juggle glasses and food and at the same time making meaningless small talk with total and frequently bibulous strangers;

standing around and, more and more, straining to hear what others are saying and shouting to make oneself heard above the din;

standing around, in fact, until everything from the back of the legs to the back of the skull becomes a repository for pain.

If ever I go among men, I come back less of a man.

—THOMAS À KEMPIS

I have discovered that all the unhappiness of men arises from one single fact, that they cannot stay quietly in their own chamber.

—BLAISE PASCAL

He never entered his room without switching on the TV and turning up the volume until the walls reverberated.

What demons, I wonder, was he trying to stifle with that incessant barrage of sound?

Faces along the bar
Cling to their average day:
The lights must never go out,
The music must always play...
Lest we should see where we are,
Lost in a haunted wood,
Children afraid of the night
Who have never been happy or
good.

—W. H. AUDEN
"September 1, 1939," *in Collected Poems of*
W. H. Auden

Amusement. It seems an innocent word. But, literally, the word (a-musement) means mindlessness.

In that original sense, an amused person is one who has stopped thinking, one who has disengaged his mind. Millions long for immortality who don't know what to do on a rainy Sunday afternoon.

—SUSAN ERTZ
In *1,911 Best Things Anybody Ever Said,*
Robert Byrne, compiler

A crowded, stuffy room
a buzz of conversation
then, suddenly, silence
but not for long
within seconds
someone speaks up

blurts out a word
relevant or not
and awkward silence
thank God, yields
to comfortable chatter

Silence is a frightening thing.
Silence leaves us at the mercy of
the noise within us. We hear the
fears that need to be faced. We
hear, then, the angers that need
to be cooled. We hear the emptiness that needs to be filled. We
hear the cries for humility and
reconciliation and centeredness.
We hear ambition and arrogance

and attitudes of uncaring awash
in the shallows of the soul.

—JOAN D. CHITTISTER
Wisdom Distilled from the Daily

A clergyman close to the breaking point came to see psychiatrist Carl Jung. The man said he had been working fourteen hours a day for months on end and his nerves were a shambles. His hands trembled uncontrollably. What should he do?

Jung's prescription was simple.

His patient was to work no more than eight hours a day. He was to get eight hours of sleep a night and spend the remaining eight hours in quietness in his study.

Pleased that he could continue with a more or less normal life, the clergyman went home hopeful that his problems would soon be over.

On that first day the minister worked only eight hours. At supper he explained the program to his wife, then went into his study, closed the door, and spent several hours playing some Chopin études and reading a Hermann Hesse novel. The next evening was much the same, only this time it was Thomas Mann's *Magic Mountain* and a Mozart sonata.

The results of the new approach? None. So again the minister went to see Jung, but this time complaining that there had been no improvement. His nerves were as bad as ever. Jung inquired into his patient's handling of the two previous days, heard the details, then shook his head.

"I'm afraid you don't understand," he said. "I don't want you with Hermann Hesse or Thomas Mann, or even Chopin and Mozart. I want you all alone with yourself."

There was a gasp. "Oh, but I can't think of any worse company!"

Jung's quiet reply: "And yet this is the self you inflict on others fourteen hours a day."

———

They intoxicate themselves with work so they won't see how they really are.

—ALDOUS HUXLEY

I find that after a time away from home, a time crammed with activity, I need several days to work my now super-charged self back into the quietness.

Quietness, it seems, is easy to abandon but hard to recover; quietness is a not a natural state. On the contrary, it is in a sense "a state of grace" and, as such, something we resist, something we achieve—or re-achieve—only through persistent effort.

But then isn't this what the doctrine of original sin is all about—the fact that goodness, any kind of goodness, tends to go against the grain?

Life without silent space is not life at all. If we're accustomed to leave the TV on in empty rooms while we work to the blur of the sounds it siphons through the house or we can't wash dishes without the radio playing; if we're never alone for a minute of the day and we never just stand and watch a flower grow; if we can't drive across town without the car tape recorder blaring and if sitting in a chair in silence for thirty min-utes a day simply thinking, thinking, thinking is one of the more painful possibilities we can imagine, then silence may be exactly what we need to wash away the frenetic energy of life and still its storms.

—JOAN D. CHITTISTER
Wisdom Distilled from the Daily

In his book *Solitude*, psychiatrist Anthony Storr states that "the capacity of the individual to make mature relationships on equal terms" is a fundamental characteristic of emotional maturity. But, he says, there is another such characteristic, one seldom recognized but no less important: "the capacity to be alone."

Our language has wisely sensed the two sides of being alone. It has created the word *loneliness* to express the pain of being alone. And it has created the word *solitude* to express the glory of being alone.

—PAUL TILLICH
In Leo Buscaglia, *Bus 9 to Paradise*

Homes are being built constantly. Why not insist that a little inner sanctuary be put into the plans, a small place where any family member could go to be alone and silent? What's to stop us? The money? We build elaborate play rooms and family rooms and think it well worth the expense. If you already own a home consider enclosing a little section of the garage or patio. If you live in an apartment be creative and find other ways to allow for solitude. I know of one family that has a special chair; whenever anyone sits in it he or she is saying, "Please don't bother me, I want to be alone."

—RICHARD J. FOSTER
Celebration of Discipline

We must reserve a little backshop, all our own, entirely free, wherein to establish our true liberty and principal retreat and solitude.

—MICHEL MONTAIGNE

When I sit here alone in the mornings—reading, pondering and writing—I may not be doing a world of good. But at least I am doing no harm to my environment, my neighbors, myself.

It also occurs to me that in a frequently angry, destructive society, simple harmlessness has much to commend it.

Primum non nocere. First of all, do no harm.

—LATIN MEDICAL PROVERB

He heaped scorn on the old-time Sabbath. "How puritanical! How repressive!"

Yes, but if people everywhere were to spend one day in seven in quietness, what a difference it would make in global energy consumption—not to mention all the other benefits.

All civil mankind have agreed in leaving one day for contemplation against six for practice.

—RALPH WALDO EMERSON

Nicholas Herman of Lorraine was a lowly and unlearned man, a footman and soldier who was converted and, in 1666, became a lay brother among the barefooted Carmelites in Paris.

Brother Lawrence, as he was now known, spent the rest of his life working in the monastery kitchen. But even there, amid the clatter of pots and pans, he became such an exemplar of pure, shining serenity that people from far and wide, prelates and nobles included, came to draw on his goodness and grace.

Wrote his biographer: "His very countenance was edifying, such a sweet and calm devotion appearing in it as could not but affect the beholders. And it was observed that in the greatest hurry of business in the kitchen he still preserved his recollection and heavenly-mindedness. He was never hasty nor loitering, but did each thing in its season, with an even, uninterrupted composure and tranquillity of spirit. 'The time of business,' said he, 'does not with me differ from the time of prayer, and in the noise and clatter of the kitchen, while several persons are at the same time calling for different things, I possess God in as great tranquillity as if I were upon my knees at the blessed sacrament.'"

———————

A farmer's wife with eight children and appeals pressing in on her from every quarter, she was busy morning, noon, and night. Amazingly, though, even in the most hectic times she was never flustered, irritated, upset; she remained serenity personified.

To me her life said this: no matter how much commotion there is on the outside, there can be quietness within.

Quiet minds cannot be perplexed or frightened, but go on in fortune or misfortune at their own private pace, like a clock during a thunderstorm.

—ROBERT LOUIS STEVENSON

A confession: I see in myself a tendency to be overly quiet, a tendency to be alone in my study when I should be out and involved.

I need to be reminded that, with the exception of love, every virtue carried too far becomes a vice.

The solution for me, surely, is neither in total acceptance of the world, nor in total renunciation of it. I must find a balance some-where, or an alternating rhythm

between these two extremes; a
swinging of the pendulum
between solitude and communion, between retreat and return.

—ANNE MORROW LINDBERGH
Gift from the Sea

Think what a better world it
would be if we all—the whole
world—had cookies and milk
about three o'clock every afternoon and then lay down with our
blankies for a nap.

—ROBERT FULGHUM
All I Really Need to Know I Learned in
Kindergarten

Slow me down, Lord!
Ease the pounding of my heart by
   the quieting of my mind.
Steady my hurried pace
With a vision of the eternal
   reach of time.
Give me, amidst the confusion of my day,
The calmness of the everlasting hills.
Break the tension of my
   nerves
With the soothing music of
   the singing streams that
   live in my memory.
Help me to know the magi-
   cal restoring power of
   sleep.
Teach me the art of taking

minute vacations of slow-
ing down:
To look at a flower;
To chat with an old friend or
make a new one;
To pat a stray dog; to watch
a spider build a web;
To smile at a child; or to
read a good book.
Remind me each day
That the race is not always
to the swift;
That there is more to life
Than increasing its speed.

—ORIN L. CRANE
In *A Pocket Full of Prayers*, Ralph L. Woods,
editor

Peace
is hallowed
by its quietness
war
damned
by its din.

———

Suffer us not to mock ourselves
with falsehood
Teach us to care, and not to
   care
Teach us to sit still.

—T. S. ELIOT
"Ash-Wednesday," in *The Complete Poems
and Plays*

Love

$\int$ see them often in the summertime. Both he and she are middle-aged, unmarried, and illiterate. Both are among the poorest of our community's poor.

I see them sitting on a park bench, sitting there quietly and, it seems, deeply contented in their friendship, their togetherness.

Seeing them, I recognize that my own friends—not my acquaintances but my friends—are those with whom there is no need to chatter, those with whom I can spend long periods in companionable silence.

I recognize, too, that such silences constitute one of friendship's essential components and, in their own way, one of life's warmest blessings.

Infatuation is
a din of emotions;
it is everything from
cries of joy to
moans of longing to
howls of misery.

Love, though,
transcends the clamor.
Love is quiet and,
in its quietness,
solid, steady
and strong.

46

In the worst of marriages
there is silence, a grim and
oppressive silence that be-
clouds the whole relationship.

I think of a couple who still
share the same home but so
loathe each other that sometimes there is no speech; there
is only an exchange of notes.

In the best of marriages
there is also silence; there are
times in which nothing is said,
and yet there is an almost palpable contentment and affection—not to mention some sur-
prising interchanges.

Says one member of such a
couple, breaking the silence, "I

was thinking..." Says the other, delightedly, "Funny, I was just thinking exactly the same thing!"

A temple commands silence. In a soaring cathedral we speak only in whispers, if at all.

A person, too, is a temple.

"Do you not know," said Paul, "that you are God's temple and that God's spirit dwells in you?" (1 Corinthians 6:19)

As long as we remain outside the temple of the person, as long as our relationship is merely superficial, there is noise; there is chatter and laughter. In those rare moments, however, when the other person admits us into the

heart of his or her being, into
the "holy of holies," there is no
noise; there is only silence, a
silence that borders on worship.

K. was in her 50s, I remember, a poised and intelligent
woman. As some saw it, she
had everything: an elegant
home, a successful and devoted
husband, children and grand-
children of whom any mother
would have been proud. Yet
there she was, being treated for
alcoholism in the psychiatric
ward of a metropolitan hospital.
Bit by bit, she was drinking herself to death.

We talked and after a while,
for the first time, she lowered
her guard and admitted me into

her inmost being, her soul. It was a place, if one can call it that, in which we said next to nothing, a place in which a gush of words would have been a desecration, a place in which our deep and wordless encounter was, in reality, an encounter with the Eternal.

Afterward, reflecting on our *meeting,* as Martin Buber would have put it, I realized anew that only when chatter has been transcended, only when there is a profound quietness both without and within, only then can we meet and know—and love— one another at the deepest level of our being.

(K. died only two weeks after

our meeting. I shared in her funeral.)

Do not the most moving moments of our lives find us without words?

—MARCEL MARCEAU

Every word is like an unnecessary stain on silence and nothingness.

—SAMUEL BECKETT

------

*O*ften," said H., "in my dealings with grief-stricken people,

I'd find myself at an utter loss for words, words that wouldn't sound trite, hollow, contrived.

"At first, I used to feel that I was failing those people. But gradually I came to see that there are times when our need is not for words but for the quiet presence of someone who aches with us, someone who shares our pain."

———

Communication is the most complete when it proceeds from the smallest number of words, and indeed of syllables.

—JACQUES BARZUN

The most precious things in
speech are pauses.

—RALPH RICHARDSON

A soft answer
turns away wrath"
(or perhaps better,
no answer at all.)

To forbear replying to an unjust
reproach, and overlook it with a
generous or, if possible, with an
entire neglect of it, is one of the
most heroic acts of a great mind.

—JOSEPH ADDISON

*B*lessed is the person
who quietly defuses
an escalating argument
by waiving his right
to the last word.

---

*J*esus, we are told, was
entertained by two sisters, Mary
and Martha. Mary sat listening
to Jesus while Martha, all busy-
ness, bustled around the
kitchen, then complained that
her sister was doing nothing to
help. Surprisingly, though, it
was Mary whom Jesus com-
mended.

Pondering the incident, I am reminded that "doing good" on a large scale is in some cases a substitute, a compensation for the inability to love individual people.

I am reminded also of a beautiful young woman, a renowned peace activist, I once hosted for an afternoon. I remember how much I looked forward to our meeting. I remember too my disappointment when I found myself dealing with a crusader of the angriest and most arrogant kind—a woman who, in fact, was arrested only hours after we parted company. The charge? Kicking a policeman in the groin.

Next I turn to my files, where I find the words of Linus of "Peanuts" fame: "I love mankind—It's *people* I can't stand!"

Also there are John Updike's lines: "Felicia had a consider-able love for people in the abstract but when actual cases got too close to her she tended to hold her nose."

————————

So whenever you give alms, do not sound a trumpet before you, as the hypocrites do in the syna-gogues and in the streets, so that they may be praised by others. Truly I tell you, they have received their reward. But when you give alms, do not let your left hand know what your right hand is doing, so that your alms may be done in secret; and your Father who sees in secret will reward you.

—MATTHEW 6:2-4 (NRSV)

⎯⎯⎯

J am told that loneliness in our society has reached pandemic proportions; everywhere people are starved for love. I am told also that loneliness can—and in countless cases does—have the most devastat-

ing effects on the human body
and soul; loneliness can be,
literally, a killer.

I wonder, though, if it is true
that quietness is basic to love,
does it not follow that the loneliness, the absence of love, we
see everywhere is attributable,
at least in part, to the frenetic
activity, the sheer noisiness of
our age?

Which is to say, it may well
be that if we were to go more
deeply into the quietness, if we
were to allow quietness (or
Quietness) itself to become our
friend, our loneliness would
largely disappear.

Thomas Merton, a Trappist
monk who spent a large part of

his adult life in a Kentucky her-
mitage, wrote these words in
his diary: "It is in deep solitude
that I find the gentleness with
which I can truly love my broth-
ers. The more solitary I am, the
more affection I have for them.
It is pure affection and filled
with reverence for the solitude
of others."

Increasingly, Merton came to
see that contemplative solitude,
far from separating him from
others, brought him into a
deeper communion with them.

Effectiveness

In 1953 Jack Lemmon came to Hollywood to make his first film, *It Should Happen to You*, co-starring with Judy Holliday. The director was George Cukor. During the first rehearsals, Cukor, after each of Lemmon's tries, would cry, "Less, less, less!" Lemmon, frustrated and bewildered, finally broke out with, "Don't you want me to act at *all*?"

"Dear boy," said Cukor, "you're beginning to understand."

—CLIFTON FADIMAN, editor
The Little, Brown Book of Anecdotes

*O*nce, years ago, I decided to do some painting, something I hadn't done in decades. My subject? A lighthouse on a bleak, windswept point. Working quickly, I sketched in the details and, almost as quickly, using watercolors, filled in the colors. In a mere couple of hours, much to my delight, my picture was completed.

Encouraged by that first small success, I set out to paint a second picture. "But this time," I told myself, "I'm going to produce a minor masterpiece." With that in mind, I bought a large canvas, spent hours in the draft-

ing process and went to work. I
fussed over every move and
labored over every detail. I was
meticulousness personified.
Unfortunately, however, my picture was a failure. I consigned it
to the garbage can and began
again. But this time too I found
that the more I struggled over
my creation, the more frustrated and dissatisfied I became.
Once again my would-be masterpiece ended up with the rest of
the household rubbish. But as if
that weren't enough, I did the
same thing still another time—
proof, I suppose, of my stub-
born failure to recognize that in
art, as in so many areas of life,
excessive effort is self-defeating.

In 1925 the *New Yorker* began publication. James Thurber, then a newspaperman, submitted several humorous pieces each entailing hours of toil. All were rejected.

A friend suggested that perhaps the articles were too studied, too labored. Perhaps if he were more spontaneous, he would stand a better chance.

"Agreed," said Thurber, and decided on a different approach. Having settled on a subject for his next submission, he set his alarm clock to ring in forty-five minutes and began writing. Three-quarters of an hour later he shut off the alarm, added a few closing words, and promptly mailed his material. Days later he received an enthusiastic letter of acceptance.

———

F. was an extraordinarily successful salesman and also one of the kindest of men. "I learned long ago," he once told me, "that it isn't the pushy, aggressive person who shines in sales. It's the more quiet and easygoing individual. Basically, I suppose, people don't like being dominated—by a salesman or by anyone else."

Dietrich Bonhoeffer and
John Bunyan
George Fox and
Feodor Dostoyevsky
Mohandas Gandhi and Paul
in prison, of all places,
made enormous contributions
to the life of the world

Inspector Japp, Agatha
Christie's bluff and busy policeman, is forever running around
in the wake of a murder, check-
ing out suspects, conducting
tests, digging for clues. Hercule
Poirot, on the other hand—the

rotund little Belgian detective—
is a devout believer in sitting at
home as much as possible and
letting "the little grey cells" do
their job. Hercule Poirot, who in
the end is always successful,
sits and ponders and waits.

In my own life there has
been something of a shift in
fairly recent years. I have
become a little less like Japp
and a little more like Poirot.

In my writing, for instance, I
used to believe that I had to
work my way through dozens
of bookstores and libraries; I
had to interview scores of people and in the process drive
hundreds, even thousands, of
miles. More and more, though, I

see that writing, for me at least, is largely a matter of hospitality. I see that what I need to do is simply and quietly go about my everyday life—the walks, the reading, the conversations—then just as quietly sit back and allow that life to speak, which amazingly, it does in a thousand and one ways.

When Leonardo da Vinci was painting "The Last Supper" in the church of Santa Maria delle Grazie in Milan, he spent many hours in apparent idleness out in the cloister, much to the annoyance of the monks who were paying for his services. Eventually a delegation went to the artist and complained that the church was not getting its money's worth. Leonardo heard them out, then explained simply, "When I pause the longest, I make the most telling strokes with my brush."

Every now and then, go away, take a little relaxation, because when you come back to your work, your judgment will be surer. To remain constantly at work will cause you to lose power of judgment. Go some distance away from it, because then the work appears smaller and more of it can be taken in at a glance, and a lack of harmony or proportion is more readily seen.

—LEONARDO DA VINCI

I try to remember his name. I try and try but without success. Finally I give up the attempt and go on with my business. Then, an hour or so later, the Aha Phenomenon, illumination! All of a sudden and all on its own, the elusive name pops up out of my unconscious mind and presents itself for my use.

Good and quickly seldom meet.

—ENGLISH PROVERB

I will suggest that healthy personality involves a balance between receptivity and manipulation, between wonder and action.

—SAM KEEN
Apology for Wonder

There is,"
he said,
"both a time
for bearing down
and a time
for backing off."

In the final analysis, to ease up is to trust. It is to trust in oneself, in others, in life; it is to trust in "the process," in tomorrow, in the Eternal.

Granted, trust can be an invitation to trouble. But, say the sages and saints, it can also be—and often is—an invitation to tremendous rewards.

Walking

*S*ome exercise
to the pulse of
blaring music,
pounding feet and
a thudding heart,
but I take
a quieter way: I go walking,
often for miles
and am blessed
in every outing.

For starters, we've got to learn to
appreciate the value of physical
activity that has nothing to do
with putting on a sweat suit or
counting sit-ups, push-ups, or

heart rates. We've got to realize that there's health to be had in simple around-the-house chores and in simple pleasures such as a game of badminton or a leisurely stroll to watch the sunset. New research is showing that not only have the austere standards of the aerobics crusade been tough to meet, but they've been downright wrong. Simple movement can help protect against heart disease whether it produces a "target heart rate" or not. Exercise gotten in bits and pieces can "count" as much as exercise gotten in large sweat-producing chunks. Body fat can be burned by walking a dog as well as by running a marathon.... Yes, strenuous exercise has benefits, but it has no monopoly on those benefits. *Moderate* physical activity, a healthy diet, a healthy weight, and an optimistic, nonhostile approach to life can do all that an aerobic exercise program can do—and more.

—BRYANT A. STAMFORD
AND PORTER SHIMER
Fitness Without Exercise

At the beginning of his or her career, every medical practitioner takes the Hippocratic oath, named after Hippocrates, the most celebrated physician in ancient Greece and also, in a sense, the father of modern medicine. "Walking," claimed Hippocrates, "is man's best medicine."

Above all, do not lose your desire to walk: every day I walk myself into a state of well-being and walk away from every illness; I have walked myself into my best thoughts, and I know of no thought so burdensome that one cannot walk away from it....The more one sits still, the closer one comes to feeling ill.... Thus if one just keeps on walking, everything will be all right.

—SØREN KIERKEGAARD

George Macaulay Trevelyan, the eminent English historian who died in 1962 at the age of 86, was a prodigious walker and a devout believer in the healing effects of his favorite pastime.

"I have two doctors, my left leg and my right," Trevelyan wrote in *Clio, a Muse*. "When body and mind are out of gear (and those twin parts of me live at such close quarters that the one always catches melancholy from the other), I know that I shall have only to call in my doctors and I shall be well again."

I find that nothing
so generates ideas
for my writing
as mile after mile
of solitary walking.

Aristotle started his Peripatetic school in 335 B.C. It was so named after his habit of walking up and down (*peripaton*) the paths of the Lyceum in Athens, while thinking and lecturing. His walking/thinking productions included works on zoology, physics, and metaphysics, rhetoric (in the original sense of

the word—the art of persuasive
speaking and writing), and
logic.... He stopped walking only
when he died in 322 B.C., the
same year as Demosthenes who
composed his famous orations
while walking on a beach. Both of
these gentlemen had studied
under Plato who paced up and
down in his outdoor schoolroom
—an olive grove. Prior to Plato,
Socrates had wandered around
the streets of Athens in search of
truth.

—GERALD DONALDSON

Jean Jacques Rousseau, the
eighteenth-century French

philosopher who maintained that the world would be a better place were we all to return to a natural state, claimed that walking was the source of his best ideas. "Never have I thought so much," he said, "never have I realized my own existence so much, been so much alive, been so much myself if I may say so, as in those journeys which I have made alone and on foot. Walking has something in it which animates and heightens my ideas: I can scarcely think when I stay in one place; my body must be set a-going if my mind is to work."

One of William Wordsworth's

admirers called at the poet's house in England's Lake District and, since the master of the home was out, asked a maid if he might see the study where Wordsworth's immortal lines were written. Replied the maid, "Here is his library, but his study is out of doors."

In his works, Wordsworth himself often refers to the inspiration he received on his walking excursions. A dedicated walker, he was credited with averaging ten miles a day and 185,000 miles during the eighty years of his lifetime. At sixty, reputedly, he was as fit as he had been at twenty.

James A Michener, a prolific author and dedicated walker, tells in his *Sports in America* of an experience he had as a student in Scotland. "On one heroic effort, which gained me some credit in my university crowd, I hiked across Scotland in one unbroken trip.... It was this long walk that committed me to constant hiking, and for the past twenty-five years, whenever I have been at home, I have left my desk almost every afternoon to walk with our dogs through the woods that surround the small plot of ground on which we live."

Michener goes on to say that his walking affects his ability to work. "When my writing goes poorly it is always because I have not walked enough, for it is on these uneventful and repetitious walks that I do my best thinking."

Listening

I have just hung up; why did he call?
I don't know.... Oh! I get it....
I talked a lot and listened very
little.

Forgive me, Lord, it was a
monologue
and not a dialogue.
I explained my idea
and did not get his;
since I didn't listen, I learned nothing,
since I didn't listen, I didn't help,
since I didn't listen,
we didn't communicate.

Forgive me, Lord,
for we were connected
and now we are cut off.

—MICHEL QUOIST
In *The Oxford Book of Prayer*, George
Appleton, editor

*S*he was young, gifted, and beautiful, married to an eminently successful man. But there she was, in my office, in tears.

"I have everything," she wept, "the car, the house, the clothes, everything. But there's one thing I don't have."

I waited.

"I don't have someone who will hear me out, someone with whom I can share the deepest places in my life."

It was, finally, a haunting cry: "I so desperately want to be known! Do you understand? I want to be *known!*"

*M*acaulay," said Lord Cockburn, "suffers from the vice of over-talking and conse-quently of under-listening."

Dear Folks,

Thank you for everything, but I am going to Chicago to try and start some kind of new life.

You asked me why I did those things and why I gave you so much trouble, and the answer is easy for me to give you, but I am wondering if you will understand.

Remember when I was about six or seven and I used to want

you to just listen to me? I remember all the nice things you gave me for Christmas and my birthday and I was really happy with the things—about a week— at the time I got the things, but the rest of the time during the year I really didn't want presents, I just wanted all the time for you to listen to me like I was somebody who felt things too, because I remember even when I was young I felt things. But you said you were busy.

Mom, you are a wonderful cook, and you had everything so clean and you were tired so much from doing all those things that made you busy; but, you know something, Mom? I would have liked crackers and peanut butter

just as well if you had only sat
down with me a while during the
day and said to me: "Tell me all
about it so I can maybe help you
understand!"

And when Donna came I
couldn't understand why everyone made so much fuss because I
didn't think it was my fault that
her hair is curly and her skin so
white, and she doesn't have to
wear glasses with such think
lenses. Her grades were better
too, weren't they?

If Donna ever has children, I
hope you will tell her to just pay
some attention to the one who
doesn't smile very much because
that one will really be crying
inside. And when she's about to

bake six dozen cookies, to make sure first, that the kids don't want to tell her about a dream or a hope or something, because thoughts are important too, to small kids even though they don't have so many words to use when they tell about what they have inside them.

I think that all the kids who are doing so many things that grown-ups are tearing out their hair worrying about are really looking for somebody that will have time to listen a few minutes and who really and truly will treat them as they would a grown-up who might be useful to them, you know—polite to them. If you folks had ever said to me:

"Pardon me," when you inter-
rupted me, I'd have dropped dead!

If anybody asks you where I
am, tell them I've gone looking
for somebody with time because
I've got a lot of things I want to
talk about.

Love to all,

Your Son

(A boy with a record as a juvenile
delinquent)

—ROBERT RAINES
Creative Brooding

Altogether I know hundreds
of people. But of that multitude

there are only a handful who
consistently probe, search,
draw me out.

Why? Is it that people who
genuinely want to listen are a
rare breed? Or is it, as J. recent-
ly suggested, that people sense
in me an unwillingness to open
up?

Pondering J.'s comment, it
occurs to me that maybe there
would be more good confessors
if there were more good con-
fessers. Maybe the dearth of
good listeners in our society is
partly attributable to the dearth
of openness and honesty in
human relationships.

*S*ure," he said, "analysis has been expensive, but I'm not complaining.

"After all, where else could I find someone who would listen indefinitely—listen, in fact, for three years running?"

(But what if even the psychiatrist won't listen? As in the case of the woman who complained about her therapist to a widely syndicated columnist: "He talks to me endlessly about his house which he dislikes because it is too small. He has confided that his children are maladjusted because he overreacts to them. . . . I know, too, that his

wife has an unhealthy attach-
ment to her father. Yesterday all
I did was listen. . . . I'm beginning to think I am the therapist
and he is the patient.")

The healing effect of a good
listener is, in some cases,
equal to that of a trained psy-
chotherapist, says a study by
Hans Strupp and Suzanne Hadley,
psychologists at Vanderbilt
University in Nashville,
Tennessee, and the National
Institute of Mental Health in
Rockville, Maryland, respective-
ly. The team found that a group
of patients treated by college

professors showed the same amount of improvement as a similar group treated by experienced psychotherapists....

The psychologists do not suggest that good listening takes the place of professional counseling. They do point out that listening contributes to establishing an understanding relationship that may be a vital part of the emotional healing process.

—JEAN PERRY
From *New York Daily News,* reprinted in
Reader's Digest

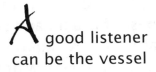

A good listener
can be the vessel

into which we empty
our disquieting woes.

One friend, one person who is
truly understanding, who takes
the trouble to listen to us as we
consider our problem, can change
our whole outlook on the world.

—ELTON MAYO
In Robert Veninga, *A Gift of Hope*

I was immensely fortunate: in
my early forties, happily married,
in the best of health, and serv-
ing a large congregation in the
most affluent area of Montreal.

Professionally, I had arrived; I was a success. But even so, I was downright miserable. Why? I didn't know. Try as I would, I couldn't identify my basic problem with the ministry.

Late one evening I was pouring out my troubles to Phyl—a superb listener—when I happened to use the term "passive-dependent." Those two words stopped me abruptly and, seconds later, sparked an enormous insight. For the first time, I saw. I saw that at a deep, unconscious level I had been bitterly resenting my congregation. Naturally, I had pretended to all concerned, including myself, that I loved them. But in point of fact I had come close to hating them. The reason? I had been far too dependent on them.

I had, of course, been financially dependent on them—after all, it was they who paid my salary. But also, I now saw, I had been emotionally dependent on them; I had seen them as my primary source of acceptance and approval. In short, I had looked to them for security, both financial and emotional.

My feelings actually were much like those of an unhappy adolescent toward his parents. I loved them, yes, to a degree. But I also resented them and longed to be free of them.

I saw too a fact that made a radical difference in my ministry: I could truly love a congregation, not to mention love myself, only when I was emotionally independent, spiritually free.

But now the question: would that insight have come if someone had not been listening, listening intently? I doubt it.

To listen well is as powerful a means of influence as to talk well.

—CHINESE PROVERB

Someone who is filled with ideas, concepts, opinions and convictions cannot be a good host. There is no inner space to listen, no openness to discover the gift of the other. It is not difficult to see how those who "know it all" can kill a conversation and prevent an interchange of ideas.

—HENRI J. M. NOUWEN
Reaching Out

A good host not only has to be poor in mind but also poor in heart. When our heart is filled with prejudices, worries, jealousies, there is little room for a stranger.

—HENRI J. M. NOUWEN
Reaching Out

There is a grace of kind listening,
as well as of kind speaking. Some
men listen with an abstracted air,
which shows that their thoughts
are elsewhere. Or they seem to
listen, but by wide answers and
irrelevant questions show that they
have been occupied with their own
thoughts, as being more interesting, at least in their own estima-
tion, than what you have been
saying. Some listen with a kind
of importunate ferocity which
makes you feel that you are being
put upon trial, and that your
auditor expects beforehand that
you are going to tell him a lie, or
to be inaccurate, or to say something of which he will disapprove,
and that you must mind your

expressions. Some interrupt, and will not hear you to the end, and then forthwith begin to talk to you about a similar experience which has befallen themselves, making your case only an illustration of their own. Some, meaning to be kind, listen with such a determined, lively, violent attention that you are at once made uncomfortable, and the charm of the conversation is at an end. Many persons whose manners will stand the test of speaking, break down under the trial of listening.... Those who govern others must take care to be kind listeners, or else they will soon offend God and fall into secret sins.

—FREDERICK WILLIAM FABER

*E*mma Bland was one of the purest, most gracious human beings I have ever known. Emma was, in short, a saint.

At the age of ninety-six, she was in hospital with a cracked hip and a broken leg, the results of a fall in a convalescent hospital where she had been recovering from still another fall. She was in traction, unable to move and in constant pain.

"When I first came here," said Emma in the course of our conversation, "I felt terribly useless. I felt that God had more for me to do than just lie flat on my back all day. So I asked him to use me in some helpful way.

"At the time," she went on, "there was another patient in that bed over there. She was—well, she wasn't quite right; she was a little disturbed.

"Anyway, she began coming over to my bedside. She'd talk and talk, oh, sometimes for an hour, maybe more. All I did, really, was just listen. But one day she told me how much I helped her just by listening. She was so grateful.

"Now I'm praying," said Emma, "that God will open up a way by which I can help someone else."

LISTENING

The first duty of love is to listen.

—PAUL TILLICH

———————

Listening and love are clearly of a piece.

—JOAN D. CHITTISTER
Wisdom Distilled from the Daily

———————

Creativity

Archimedes lounging
in his tub
Watts contemplating
a boiling kettle
Newton sprawled out
under an apple tree
men woolgathering
nothing more
when suddenly
out of the blue
truth burst
into their lives.

Insights seem to flourish best
when the thinker is apparently
wasting time.

—J. ROBERT OPPENHEIMER

It takes a lot of time to be a genius; you have to sit around so much doing nothing, really doing nothing.

—ERNEST HEMINGWAY

Certain springs are tapped only when we are alone. The artist knows he must be alone to create; the writer, to work out his thoughts; the musician, to compose; the saint, to pray.

—ANNE MORROW LINDBERGH
Gift from the Sea

All beneficent and creative power gathers itself together in silence, ere it issues out in might. Force itself indeed is naturally silent and only makes itself heard, if at all, when it strikes upon obstructions to bear them away as it returns to equilibrium again. The very hurricane that roars over land and ocean flits noiselessly through spaces where nothing meets it. The blessed sunshine says nothing as it warms the vernal earth, tempts out the tender grass, and decks the field and forest in their glory.... Nowhere can you find any beautiful work, any noble design, any durable endeavor, that was not matured in long and patient silence ere it speak out in its accomplishment.

—JAMES MARTINEAU

The greatest ideas, the most profound thoughts, and the most
beautiful poetry are born from
the womb of silence.

—WILLIAM A. WARD

For not, surely, by deliberate
effort of thought does a man grow
wise. The truths of life are not
discovered by us. At moments
unforeseen, some gracious influence descends upon the soul,
touching it to an emotion which,
we know not how, the mind
transmutes into thought. This
can happen only in a calm of the
senses, a surrender of the whole
being to passionless contempla-

tion. I understand, now, the intellectual mood of the quietest.

—GEORGE GISSING

Klee realized, perhaps more clearly than any artist since Goethe, that all effort is in vain if it is forced: that the essential formative process takes place below the level of consciousness.

—HERBERT READ
A Concise History of Modern Painting

It is by long obedience and hard work that the artist comes to unforced spontaneity and consummate mastery. Knowing that he can never create anything on his own account, out of the top layers, so to speak, of his personal consciousness, he submits obediently to the workings of "inspiration"; and knowing that the medium in which he works has its own self-nature, which must not be ignored or violently overridden, he makes himself its patient servant and, in this way, achieves perfect freedom of expression. But life is also an art, and the man who would become a consummate artist in living must follow, on all levels of his being, the same procedure as that by which the painter or sculptor or any other craftsman comes to his own more limited perfection.

—ALDOUS HUXLEY
The Perennial Philosophy

Happiness

A happy life must be to a great
extent a quiet life, for it
is only in an atmosphere of quiet
that true joy can live.

—BERTRAND RUSSELL

Everybody strains after happiness,
and the result is that nobody's
happy.

—ALDOUS HUXLEY
Point Counter Point

*M*axim Gorki, the Russian writer, was once taken to see Coney Island. *What better way,* his hosts thought, *to show him America at play?* It turned out to be a busy afternoon for the Russian visitor. He was walked for miles, plied with cotton candy and hot dogs, and shown thousands of people goggling at the exhibits in the palace of freaks, rocketing around on the rollercoaster, and otherwise indulging their appetite for excitement and fun. After it was all over, his friends asked Gorki how he had liked it. His perceptive,

disquieting comment: "What a
sad people you must be!"

The search for happiness is one of
the chief sources of unhappiness.

—ERIC HOFFER
In J. B. W., *A New Day*

If only we'd stop trying to be
happy we could have a pretty
good time.

—EDITH WHARTON
In *The Penguin Dictionary of Modern
Humorous Quotations*

For centuries great mystics of all faiths have insisted that to pursue mystical ecstasy too vigorously, too greedily, is to invite a certain "false mysticism," an ecstasy which, beautiful though it may seem, is essentially Satanic and which, as such, carries the potential for madness and destruction.

Mystical rapture, they say, should be gratefully accepted when it comes our way but never aggressively pursued, because the more we pursue the gifts of God, ecstasy included, the more we invite their very opposite.

126

A paradoxical fact: the more ardently we pursue ecstasy, the more likely we are to end up oppressed by misery; the more aggressively we seek heaven, the better our chances of ending up in hell.

———————

It is the man who tries hard to get himself newness of life who succeeds only in shutting himself up against it.

—H. A. WILLIAMS
True Resurrection

———————

If there is one thing I really believe it is that in the final summing-up each of us receives

the same amount of happiness. I
don't mean good luck or success.
I mean that clear, sharp singing
feeling that is so rare and lasts
such a short time. If it would last
it wouldn't be happiness anymore.
If it were our daily bread we
wouldn't appreciate it.

Happiness cannot be forced or
coaxed or commanded. It comes
all by itself and everyone can be
sure to get a share. But this share
may be a little bigger if we are
ready to be happy, ready and
relaxed and willing to recognize
the rare bird when it alights in
our heart.

—VICKI BAUM
In Francis Gay, *The Friendship Book of
Francis Gay*, 1979

Happiness is like the bluebird of Maeterlinck: try to catch it and it loses its color. It's like trying to hold water in your hands. The more you squeeze it the more it runs away.

—MICHELANGEO ANTONIONI
In *The Pan Dictionary of Contemporary Quotations*

He who binds to himself a joy
Doth the wingèd life destroy;
But he who kisses the joy
as it flies
Lives in Eternity's sunrise.

—WILLIAM BLAKE

Happiness is a butterfly which, when pursued, is always just beyond your grasp, but which, if you will sit down quietly, may alight upon you.

—NATHANIEL HAWTHORNE

———

Over the years, whether explicitly or implicitly, I have heard it from hundreds of sources: "I'll be happy when..." (when I receive that raise, that promotion, that transfer).

The fact is, though, that to dwell on the *when* is to overlook the immense possibilities inherent in the *now*. William Moulton Marston, the psychologist, once asked 300 people, "What do you have to live for?" Marston was jolted by his findings: nine out of ten were simply putting in time, waiting for something to develop, a better job perhaps, a Caribbean holiday, a proposal of marriage. Nine out of ten, in their longing for the future, were failing to appreciate the present.

I believe that only one person in a thousand knows the trick of really living in the present. Most of us spend fifty-nine minutes an hour living in the past...or in a future which we either long for or dread. The only way to live is by accepting each minute as an unrepeatable miracle—which is exactly what it is.

—STORM JAMESON
In Ardis Whitman, *"Resources to Live By"*

The French speak of *le petit bonheur,* the happy little moment we experience from time to time—but could perhaps experience much more often than we do.

Earlier in his life, says Will Durant, he looked for happiness in knowledge but found disillusionment. He looked for happiness in travel and found only boredom, in wealth and found only discord and anxiety. He looked for happiness in his writing, but all he found was lassitude and fatigue. Then one day he saw, seated in a car, a woman with a sleeping child in her arms. A train came, and from the train emerged a man who walked over to the car, gently kissed the woman and even more gently, so as not to waken it, kissed the child. Driving away together, the little family left the historian dazed by the realization that even life's most ordinary moments are freighted with the potential for sheer bliss.

Look inward, for you have a last-
ing fountain of happiness at
home that will always bubble up
if you will but dig for it.

—MARCUS AURELIUS

———

"My experience," said an old
gentleman to me, "has been that
I never could succeed in getting
the special kind of happiness I
had wanted or hoped for, but that
other kinds of happiness which I
did not want and had never
hoped for were supplied to me, in
the course of life, most lavishly
and abundantly. I therefore ended
by discovering, though it took me

a long time to make the discovery, that the right way to enjoy the happiness within my reach was not to form an ideal of my own and be disappointed when it was not realized—for that it never was—but to accept the opportunities for enjoying life which were offered by life itself from year to year and from day to day. Since I took things in this temper, I have enjoyed really a great amount of happiness, though it has been of a kind entirely different from anything I ever anticipated or laid plans for when I was young."

—PHILIP GILBERT HAMERTON

An old Hasidic story tells of a poor rabbi named Rabbi Eizik, son of Yekel of Cracow, who was commanded in a dream to look for a treasure under a bridge leading to the king's palace in Prague. The rabbi dismissed the message, but after two more dreams, each with the same instructions, he obeyed; he packed his bag and left for Prague.

There, however, he found himself with a problem: the bridge was guarded day and night by soldiers. What to do? In his perplexity, the rabbi paced the site for hour after hour.

Finally, at sundown, the captain of the guard came over and asked if he could be of help. Sensing that here was a kindly man, the rabbi told him about his dream and subsequent journey.

"So," said the captain, "at the behest of a mere dream, you have worn out all that shoe leather and come all this way. Why, if I had as much faith in my dreams as you have in yours, I would have gone to Cracow to look for treasure under the stove of a Jew named Rabbi Eizik, son of Yekel. Can you imagine anything so foolish?"

Rabbi Eizik did not debate the point. He thanked the captain for his understanding, bowed, walked home, and dug up the treasure under his stove. Nor did he spend the money foolishly. He built a house of worship in which he could praise God for helping him understand that his treasure was not in some distant place; his treasure was wherever he happened to be.

———

J know a number
of extraordinarily
fulfilled people
who explore life
in such localized depth
that, for them,
the global breadth
of extensive travel
is without appeal.

*M*any a journey, born of
  restlessness,
is an attempt to compensate for
an inward odyssey, a spiritual
  pilgrimage,
that has yet to be made.

And see all sights
from pole to pole
And glance, and nod,
and bustle by,
And never once possess our soul
Before we die.

—MATTHEW ARNOLD

Will you seek afar off? You will
come back at last to things best

known to you, finding happiness,
knowledge, not in another place
but in this place... not in another
hour, but *this* hour.

—WALT WHITMAN

The next winter I sat in army
fatigues somewhere near
Anniston, Alabama, eating my
supper out of a mess kit. The
infantry training battalion that I
had been assigned to was on
bivouac. There was a cold drizzle
of rain, and everything was mud.
The sun had gone down. I was
still hungry when I finished and
noticed that a man nearby had
something left over that he was

not going to eat. It was a turnip
and when I asked him if I could
have it, he tossed it over to me. I
missed the catch, the turnip fell
to the ground, but I wanted it so
badly that I picked it up and
started eating it anyway, mud and
all. And then, as I ate it, time
deepened and slowed down again.
With a lurch of the heart that is
real to me still, I saw suddenly,
almost as if from beyond time
altogether, that not only as the
turnip good, but the mud was
good too, even the drizzle and
cold were good, even the Army
that I had dreaded for months.
Sitting there in the Alabama
winter with my mouth full of
cold turnip and mud, I could see

at least for a moment how if you ever took to heart the ultimate goodness and joy of things, even at their bleakest, the need to praise someone or something for it would be so great that you might even have to go out and speak of it to the birds of the air.

—FREDERICK BUECHNER
The Sacred Journey

Awareness

One day a traveler begged the Teacher for a word of wisdom that would guide the rest of the journey.

The Teacher nodded affably and though it was a day of silence took a sheet of paper and wrote on it a single word, "Awareness."

"Awareness?" the traveler said, perplexed. "That's far too brief. Couldn't you expand on that a bit?"

So the Teacher took the paper back and wrote: "Awareness, awareness, awareness."

"But what do those words mean?" the traveler insisted.

Finally the teacher reached for the paper and wrote, clearly and firmly, "Awareness, awareness, awareness means . . . Awareness!"

—JOAN D. CHITTISTER
Wisdom Distilled from the Daily

*O*ne of the most poignant scenes in Thornton Wilder's classic *Our Town* tells of Emily's return to Grover's Corners.

Emily, a young woman who died while giving birth, is permitted by the Stage Manager to return and relive just one day from her childhood. Her choice of days is her twelfth birthday. As it turns out, though, Emily is acutely disappointed. Members of the family are so busy, so caught up in a mass of trivia, that the sheer wonder of life goes right by them.

Finally Emily asks to be taken back, but not before saying good-bye in words that once moved me to tears: "Good-bye, Good-bye, world. Good-bye, Grover's Corners . . . Mama and Papa. Good-bye to clocks ticking . . . and Mama's sunflowers. And food and coffee. And new-ironed dresses and hot baths . . . and sleeping and waking up. Oh, earth, you're too wonderful for anybody to realize you." She then turns to the Stage Manager and asks, "Do any human beings ever realize

life while they live it? every,
every minute?"

"No," answers the Stage
Manager. "The saints and poets
maybe—they do some."

The spring blew trumpets of
    color,
  Her green sang in my brain;
I heard a blind man groping
    tap-tap with his cane.

I pitied him for his blindness
    but can I say I see?
Perhaps there walks close by a
    spirit that pities me.

AWARENESS

A spirit that sees me tapping the
   five-sensed cane of time;
Amid such unguess'd glories
   that I am worse than blind!

—HARRY KEMP

We have become so dead to feeling, so inured to wonder. The stimuli of our age have been so gross as almost to kill off the senses, or at least to dampen and mute them. Television, radio, rock-and-roll, jet planes, sonic booms, housing projects, concrete jungles, land erosion, water pollution, traffic congestion, smog, saturation advertising, 30,000 new book titles a year; we are the first generation in the history of mankind to commit suicide by orgy!

—JOHN KILLINGER
For God's Sake, Be Human

We suffer, said Kierkegaard, from "shutupness." All around us is material for wonder and joy, but instead of being open to this wealth of potential delight, we go hurrying through life with our appreciative faculties largely inoperative.

The world
will never starve for wonders
but only
for the want of wonder.

—GILBERT K. CHESTERTON

A flock of wild geese flew over philosopher Henry G. Bugbee Jr.'s home. He rushed to the window and was barely able to count them, forty-five in all, before they disappeared into the storm clouds downwind.

Later, in telling of the incident, he was confronted with a question: "If you counted them, how could you have seen them?"

(I too have found, not once but again and again, that my passion for numbers is no friend to wonder and awe.)

God does not die on the day when we cease to believe in a personal deity, but we die on the day when our lives cease to be illumined by the steady radiance, renewed daily, of a wonder, the source of which is beyond all reason.

—DAG HAMMARSKJÖLD
Markings, Leif Sjöberg & W. H. Auden, translators

Wonder," says psychologist Rollo May, "is essentially an 'opening' attitude—an awareness that there is more to life than one has yet fathomed, an experience of new vistas in life to be explored as well as new profundities to be plumbed."

I find it a comforting thought, because while I cannot deliberately conjure up a sense of wonder, I can be more "open to the world" and in so doing invite the wonder that glorifies our lives.

———————

*S*ocrates, says Plato, was convinced that wonder is the source and foundation of philosophy, which is, in turn, the highest human activity. (Plato quotes Socrates' words to Theaetetus: "I see, my dear Theaetetus, that Theodorus had a true insight into your nature when he said that you were a philosopher, for wonder is the feeling of a philosopher, and philosophy begins in wonder.")

For Aristotle, too, wonder was central to philosophy: "It is owing to their wonder that men both now begin and at first began to philosophize."

The sense of wonder,
that is our sixth sense.
And it is the natural religious
sense.

—D. H. LAWRENCE
In Sam Keen, *Apology for Wonder*

The most beautiful experience we can have is the mysterious. It is the fundamental emotion which stands at the cradle of true art and science. Whoever does not know it and can no longer wonder, no longer marvel, is as good as dead, and his eyes are dimmed. It was the experience of mystery —even if mixed with fear—that engendered religion. A knowledge of the existence of something we cannot penetrate, our perceptions of the profoundest reason and the most radiant beauty, which only in their most primitive forms are accessible to our minds—it is this knowledge and this emotion that constitutes true religiosity.

—ALBERT EINSTEIN

Whenever beauty overwhelms us,
whenever wonder
silences our chattering hopes
and worries,
we are close to worship.

—RICHARD C. CABOT
In Mark Link, *In the Stillness Is the Dancing*

The real voyage of discovery con-
sists not in seeking new land-
scapes, but in having new eyes.

—MARCEL PROUST

A mature sense of wonder does
not need the constant titillation
of the sensational to keep it alive.

It is most often called forth by a confrontation with the mysterious depth of meaning at the heart of the familiar and quotidian. Rare birds—the scarlet tanagers and indigo buntings of experience—do upon occasion delight us, but a mature sense of wonder may be evoked by starlings and English sparrows. One is reminded of the incident in *Zorba the Greek* when Zorba and the boss meet a peasant riding on a donkey.

One day, I remember, when we were making our way to the village, we met a little old man astride a mule. Zorba opened his eyes wide as he looked at the beast. *And his look was so intense that the peasant cried out in terror: "For God's sake, brother, don't give him the evil eye!" And he crossed himself.*

I turned to Zorba. "What did you do to the old chap to make him cry out like that?" I asked him.

"Me? What d'you think I did? I was looking at his mule, that's all! Didn't it strike you, boss?"

"What?"

"Well . . . that there are such things as mules in this world!"

—SAM KEEN
Apology for Wonder

—NIKOS KAZANTZAKIS
Zorba the Greek

158

Once you begin to study it, all Nature is equally interesting and equally charged with beauty. I was shown a picture of Cézanne of a blank wall of a house, which he had made instinct with the most delicate lights and colors. Now I often amuse myself when I am looking at a wall or a flat surface of any kind by trying to distinguish all the different colors and tints which can be discerned upon it, and considering whether these arise from reflections or from natural hue. You would be astonished the first time you tried this to see how many and what beautiful colors there are even in the most commonplace objects, and the more carefully and frequently you look the more variations do you perceive.

—WINSTON CHURCHILL
Thoughts and Adventures

The sculptress Louise Nevelson believed that one can live in great beauty anywhere. She made her home in the Bowery, New York City's skid row, and even there, she said, "I collect for my eye." Sitting in her dining room and looking out at the ugly building that stood across the street, she could find beauty in the varying patterns the sun and the moon reflected on its windows. She would look at a chair and say,

"The chair isn't so hot, but look at its shadow."

—ALAN LOY MCGINNIS
The Power of Optimism

In psychiatrist Viktor Frankl's classic little book *Man's Search for Meaning*, a book which tells of his life in a Nazi concentration camp, Frankl observes that, amazingly, in the degradation and horror of the camps, prisoners experienced the beauties of nature and art as never before.

One evening, says Frankl, when he was in a Bavarian camp, a prisoner came running into the building where the others were all huddled on the floor, resting and eating their ration of soup. Excitedly, the prisoner urged the others to rush out onto the assembly ground and see the beautiful sunset.

Tired though they were, the men trooped outside and stood in hushed admiration at the sight of the dazzling colors of the evening sky, colors ranging all the way from fiery red to steely blue, colors in the starkest contrast to the gray drabness of the camp itself.

After a long silence, one prisoner murmured, "How beautiful the world *could* be!"

By examining as closely and candidly as I could the life that had come to seem to me in many ways a kind of trap or dead-end street, I discovered that it really wasn't that at all. I discovered that if you really keep your eye peeled to it and your ears open, if you really pay attention to it, even such a limited and limiting life as the one I was leading on Rupert Mountain opened up onto extraordinary vistas. Taking your children to school and kissing your wife good-bye. Eating lunch with a friend. Trying to do a decent day's work. Hearing the rain patter against the window. There is no event so commonplace but that God is always present within it, always hiddenly, always leaving you room to recognize him or not to recognize him, but all the more fascinatingly because of that, all the more compellingly and hauntingly. In writing those lectures and the book they later turned into, it came to seem to me that if I were called upon to state in a few words the essence of everything I was trying to say both as a novelist and as a preacher, it would be something like this: Listen to your life. See it for the fathomless mystery that it is. In the boredom and pain of it no less than in the excitement and gladness: touch, taste, smell your way to the holy and hidden heart of it because in the last analysis all moments are key moments, and life itself is grace. What I started trying to do as a writer and as a preacher was more and more to draw on my own experience not just as a source of plot, character, illustration, but as a source of truth.

—FREDERICK BUECHNER
Now and Then

O God, we thank thee for this universe, our great home, for its vastness and its riches, and for the manifoldness of the life which teems upon it and of which we are part. We praise thee for the arching sky and the blessed winds, for the driving clouds and the constellations on high. We praise thee for the salt sea and the running water, for the everlasting hills, for the trees, and for the grass under our feet. We thank thee for our senses by which we can see the splendor of the morning, hear the jubilant songs of love, and smell the breath of the springtime. Grant us, we pray thee, a heart wide open to all this joy and beauty, and save our souls from being so steeped in care or so darkened by passion that we pass heedless and unseeing when even the thorn-bush by the wayside is aflame with the glory of God.

—AUTHOR UNKNOWN

Emptiness

My life in Connecticut, I begin to realize, lacks this quality of significance and therefore of beauty, because there is so little empty space. The space is scribbled on; the time has been filled. There are so few empty pages in my engagement pad, or empty rooms in my life in which to stand alone and find myself. Too many activities, and people, and things. Too many worthy activities, valuable things, and interesting people. For it is not merely the trivial which clutters our lives but the important as well. We can have a surfeit of treasures.

—ANNE MORROW LINDBERGH
Gift from the Sea

For me the greatest
hindrances
to quietude,
the enemies-in-chief,
are not the jackhammers
and sirens,
the high-decibel performers
and howling jets;
the enemies, rather, are
ambition, resentment,
impatience, discontent;
the enemies are not without
but within.

The war against microbes has
been largely won, but the struggle
for equanimity is being lost. It is
not just the congestion outside
us—a congestion of people and

ideas and issues—but our inner congestion that is hurting us. Our experiences come at us from so many different directions that they are never really sorted out, much less absorbed. The result is clutter and confusion. We gorge the senses and starve the sensibilities.

—NORMAN COUSINS
Human Options

Spiritual hospitality requires a certain emptiness. After all, how can we receive the gifts of truth and beauty and love if our inward selves are a crowded mass of conflicts, prejudices, anxieties, desires?

Pompey, the Roman general, barged into the Temple in Jerusalem, demanded to be shown the Holy of Holies, the inmost shrine, and was surprised to find himself in—an empty room.

———————

J was in my late thirties and, in one sense, in the best of health. I exercised each morning, strenuously. I could hike for hours and swim for miles. But at the same time something was seriously wrong: I couldn't work.

A few minutes of work and there would be a tightness in

my chest, a constriction that soon became such a relentless ache that a couple of hours later, absolutely exhausted, I would have to go back to bed. I spent my days going from bed to desk and from desk to bed, over and over again.

I went to see a physician friend. "I have no energy, no stamina," I said. "I'm working less than half time, but even so I'm wrung right out."

He put me through an exhaustive battery of tests, then shared his findings. There was nothing organically wrong. The trouble must be elsewhere. Attitudinal perhaps? Psychosomatic?

I went on with my work and

in the process, tried everything
I knew, everything from yoga
and self-analysis to fasting and
affirmative prayer. All that
resulted was that I went from
bad to worse.

Finally, one night in my study
upstairs, I fell to my knees,
driven there because I had
nowhere else to go, and in the
darkness began pouring out my
heart in silent prayer. At first,
unspoken though it was, it was
a long, agonizing wail of help-
lessness and need. From there
it drifted somehow into a confession of sin, but one far different from any I had ever
offered before. My acknowledg-
ment of some of the more obvi-

ous sins, it seemed, triggered the recognition of others, a few at first and then more and still more—sins of the spirit, most of them, profoundly subtle, overwhelming in their sheer multitude and as fetid and hideous as only sin can be.

As C. S. Lewis put it, "I found what appalled me; a zoo of lusts, a bedlam of ambitions, a nursery of fears, a harem of fondled hatreds. My name was legion."

It was a catharsis that went on and on for perhaps an hour and left me drained, it seemed, of every shred of self-esteem.

At last—still apparently following some kind of leading—I concluded the prayer by offering up the remnants of my broken, defeated being. "I can no longer manage my life," I said. "I'm giving it over to You, all of it. Do with it whatever You will."

There was no thunderclap, no blinding light. There was, though, a priceless gift: a strange ineffable peace, a healing that filled my whole being. I went to bed, slept like a child, and wakened the next morning a new person.

———

There are many programs to prepare people for service in its different forms. But seldom do we look at these programs as a train-

ing toward a voluntary poverty.
Instead we want to become better
equipped and more skillful. We
want to acquire the "tools of the
trade." But real training for service asks for a hard and often
painful process of self-emptying....
Training for service is not a training to become rich but to become
voluntarily poor; not to fulfill
ourselves but to empty ourselves;
not to conquer God but to surrender to his saving power. All this
is very hard to accept in our contemporary world, which tells us
about the importance of power
and influence. But it is important
that in this world there remain a
few voices crying out that if there
is anything to boast of, we should

boast of our weakness. Our fulfillment is in offering emptiness, our usefulness in becoming useless, our power in becoming powerless. It indeed belongs to the core of the Christian message that God did not reveal himself to us as the powerful other, unapproachable in his omniscience. Instead he came to us in Jesus Christ who "did not cling to his equality with God, but emptied himself... and became as men are; and being as all men are, he was humbler yet even to accepting death, death on a cross" (Philippians 2:6-8).

—HENRI J. M. NOUWEN
Reaching Out

There will come a day, I know,
when, the last breath drawn,
   my life will be emptied
   of life itself.
But I know too that insofar as I
   empty my life between now
and then,
   empty it of every discordant
element,
   empty it of all but love,
my deathday, devoid of terror,
   will present
   an easy drift
   into a shining eternity.

Father, to Thee I raise my whole
being, a vessel emptied of self.
Accept, Lord, this my emptiness

and so fill me with Thyself—Thy
Light, Thy Love, Thy Life—that
these Thy precious gifts may radi-
ate through me and overflow the
chalice of my heart into the heats
of all with whom I come in contact
this day, revealing unto them the
beauty of Thy Joy and Wholeness
and the serenity of Thy Peace
which nothing can destroy.

—AUTHOR UNKNOWN

My spirit bare before thee stands;
I bring no gift, I ask no sign,
I come to Thee with empty
    hands,
The surer to be filled from Thine.

—DORA GREENWELL
In *A Diary of Readings,* John Baille, compiler

Waiting

*W*hy is it that, with forebears who could miss a stagecoach and cheerfully wait days for another, we scowl and mutter imprecations while waiting for a set of lights to change from red to green?

*W*hen I see fast foods,
condensed books,
instant coffee,
speed reading,
Polaroid cameras,
quickie divorces,
same-day surgery,
microwave ovens,

supersonic transports,
I can only conclude
ours is not
a patient society.

———

Writing, for me at least, is as much a matter of waiting as it is of actual writing—waiting hours, days, and even weeks for the dawning of an idea, then more and still more waiting for the words, the right words, to give substance to the thought. Inspiration, it seems, does not come on command.

One of the marks
of maturity is the
ability to wait.
An infant cannot
wait patiently for
a need to be met.
An elderly saint
can wait quietly
forever and a day.

We must wait for God, long,
meekly, in the wind and wet, in
the thunder and lightning, in the
cold and the dark. Wait, and he
will come. He never comes to
those who do not wait. He does

not go their road. When he
comes, go with him, but go slow-
ly, fall a little behind; when he
quickens his pace, be sure of it
before you quicken yours. But
when he slackens, slacken at once;
and do not be slow only, but
silent, very silent, for he is God.

—FREDERICK W. FABER

Waiting patiently in expectation
is the foundation of the spiritual
life.

—SIMONE WEIL
First and Last Notebooks

I wait for the LORD, my soul
  waits,
and in his word I hope.

—PSALM 130:5 (NRSV)

---

*G*od knows
the hardest waiting of all
is waiting for a beloved
prodigal
to come to his or her senses.
Waiting, at its best,
is essentially trust,
trust that in time
or, if not in time
then in eternity
(in the words of
Saint Julian of Norwich),

"All shall be well and
all shall be well and
all manner of things
shall be well."

Teach us, O Father, to trust Thee
with life and with death,
And (though this is harder by far)
With the life and death of those
that are dearer to us than our life.

Teach us stillness and confident
peace
In Thy perfect will,
Deep calm of soul, and content
In what Thou wilt do with these

lives Thou hast given.
Teach us to wait and be still,
To rest in Thyself,
To hush this clamorous anxiety,
To lay in Thine arms all this
wealth Thou hast given.

Thou lovest these souls
that we love
With a love as far surpassing
our own
As the glory of noon surpasses
the gleam of a candle.
Therefore will we be still,
And trust in Thee.

—J. S. HOYLAND

Faith

Thomas Carlyle, I am told, went out to dinner and spent the entire evening haranguing the others present on the merits of silence.

I smile, but then, my smugness shattered, realize that I have done much the same thing myself: preached for twenty minutes—with magnificent inconsistency—on the text, "Be still, and know that I am God."

About to board ship for his return journey to Japan, Toyohiko Kagawa was asked about his impression of the church in North America. Kagawa's succinct reply: "Too much talk."

Several years ago I gave the University of California a sum of money that would yield at least five hundred dollars a year to be given as a prize for an essay of five hundred words. A dollar a word! There was an outcry from students and from some of the faculty: "What can one say in five hundred words?" My answer was that there is not an idea that cannot be expressed in two hundred words, and the prize allows words

enough for two and a half original
ideas.

—ERIC HOFFER
Before the Sabbath

The fewer words, the better
prayer.
—MARTIN LUTHER

You need not cry very loud;
he is nearer to us than we think.

—BROTHER LAWRENCE

---

*H*ow to reconcile
the fulminations
of fire-and-brimstone preachers
with the essential quietness
of the Eternal?

Outside noisy, inside empty.

—CHINESE PROVERB

How can you expect God to speak
in that gentle and inward voice
which melts the soul,
when you are making so much
noise
with your rapid reflections?
Be silent,
and God will speak again.

—FRANÇOIS FENELON

196

Our problem is not that we take refuge from action in spiritual things, but that we take refuge from spiritual things in action.

—MONICA FURLONG
In *The Hodder Book of Christian Quotations*

I recall a saying I read one time on a church bulletin board: "Don't just do something, *sit there!*" Perhaps the most *practical* thing that most Christians could do at this time would be to "sit there," to begin to think, to reflect, to read, to meditate.

—DOUGLAS JOHN HALL
Has the Church a Future?

What frightens me most is the glorification of activity, especially when it happens in the church. How can anything grow in us without passivity, the long, dull wait for birth?

—-MONICA FURLONG
Travelling In

In quietness and in confidence shall be your strength.

—ISAIAH 30:15 (KJV)

There is a sacred simplicity in not doing something—and not doing it well. All the great religious leaders have done it. The Buddha sat still under a tree. Jesus sat

still in a garden. Muhammad sat
still in a cave. And Gandhi and
King and thousands of others have
brought sitting still to perfection
as a powerful tool of social
change. Passive resistant, meditation, prayer—one and the same.

—ROBERT FULGHUM
It Was on Fire When I Lay Down on It

The very best and utmost attain-
ment in this life is to remain still
and let God act and speak in thee.

—MEISTER ECKHART

Settle yourself in solitude and you
will come upon Him in yourself.

—TERESA OF AVILA

The essential attitude of Platonism is aspiration or longing: the human soul, imprisoned in the shadowy, unreal world of Nature, stretches out its hands and struggles toward the beauty and reality of that which lies (as Plato says) "on the other side of existence."...In Christianity, however, the human soul is not the seeker but the sought: it is God who seeks, who descends from the other world to find and heal Man; the parable about the Good Shepherd looking for and finding the lost sheep sums it up.

—C. S. LEWIS
Studies in Medieval and Renaissance Literature

There is no other possession of God than to let oneself be possessed *by* God. Mysticism is an action in the passive.

—ALAN WATTS
Behold the Spirit

Do not entertain the notion that you ought to *advance* in your prayer. If you do, you will only find you have put on the brake instead of the accelerator. All real progress in spiritual things comes gently, imperceptibly, and is the work of God. Our crude efforts spoil it. Know yourself for the childish, limited and dependent soul you are. Remember that the only growth which matters happens without our knowledge and that trying to stretch ourselves is both dangerous and silly. Think of the Infinite Goodness, never of your own taste. Realize that the very capacity to pray at all is the free gift of Divine Love and be content with St. Francis de Sales' favorite prayer in which all personal religion is summed up. "Yes, Father! Yes, and always Yes!"

—EVELYN UNDERHILL
In *Affirmations of God and Man*, Edmund Fuller, editor

Contemplation is no less a mode of thought or reason than scientific investigation. However, it does differ in both structure and intent. The chief characteristic of contemplation is its receptive passivity. This passivity is not to be confused with inertness or languor but is, rather, the calm and disciplined effort of thought to be open to the uniqueness and novelty of its object. In contemplation, thought makes an effort to be fluid or plastic, to conform itself to the object, and to allow the object to create categories by which it will be understood. A disciplined silence is essential to contemplation in order to allow the object to speak. The obvious illustration of this type of thought would be the attentive listening involved in trying to understand another person.

—SAM KEEN
Apology for Wonder

———

"Resonance to the All," said Pierre Teilhard de Chardin, "is the keynote of pure poetry and pure religion." Such listening is akin to prayer. As Simone Weil said, "Attention is an acceptable form of prayer."

—JACOB TRAPP
The Light of a Thousand Suns

———

But as prayer and meditation develop, the whole process

usually begins to simplify. One may be content to repeat a single word like the word "Jesus." Or he may use a favorite ejaculation like "Come, Holy Spirit," repeated easily and quietly with the breathing or at one's own pace. And then the time may come when one prefers to use no words at all but simply *to be*: to be silent in the presence of the mystery. In such a state of prayer one may be unable to think because one is caught up in a peaceful wordlessness that is filled with love.

It is now that one enters the mystical silence, the *silentium mysticum* about which the Christian mystics love to talk....

In this silence the mystics

speak of maintaining a certain *awareness*, that is to say, a certain attentiveness to the presence of God who is within or around. And for them this "obscure sense of presence" is a great grace. The old theologians spoke of it as presence through love, in this way distinguishing it from physical presence or presence through knowledge. It is indeed *loving awareness*.

—WILLIAM JOHNSTON
The Mirror Mind

Drop thy still dews of quietness,
Till all our strivings cease;
Take from our souls the strain

and stress,
And let our ordered lives confess
The beauty of thy peace.

—JOHN GREENLEAF WHITTIER
The Book of Praise

The Twilight Years

A local nursing home aims at including every resident in its activities program.

I wonder, though, if we are not doing the elderly a serious disservice in filling their days with everything from sing-songs and bingo to finger-painting and bridge.

I wonder if one of their most fundamental needs is not to enter deeply into the quietness and, in that quietness, come to terms with the whole of their lives, past, present, and future as well.

I am not eager, bold
or strong—all that is past.
I am ready *not* to do,
At last, at last!

—ST. PETER CANISIUS

He who is of a calm and happy
nature will hardly feel the pres-
sure of age, but he who is of an
opposite disposition will find
youth and age equally a burden.

—PLATO

During the first part of our life,
growth is effected principally by
personal effort as we strive for

goals and achievement. During the second period of life we will only grow if we master the great art of *wu-wei* or non-action— learning to let growth take place so that we can develop to our fullness as persons.

—WILLIAM JOHNSTON
The Mirror Mind

Aging has taken its toll. I could name dozens of things I once did at least passably but now do poorly, if at all. Still, even though I can *do* less and less, I hope that, with Help, I can *be* more and more.

213

People should not consider so much what they are to do, as what they are.

—MEISTER ECKHART

I think there are some very big lessons for the old. Some old people trundle along, some old people stay alert. I feel about twelve! And the lesson I must learn is, what does it mean not to be able to do things? Everybody screams—and I include myself— "I can't do this and I can't do that" and "*Baaah!*" The lesson to be learnt is to understand the promotion from plum-easy doing to the surprisingly difficult non-activity of just *being*. Be patient, be gentle, be *nothing*. Somebody said that the real vocation of old age was to give out love. So no more doing, but being. I told an old lady in a home this and she said, "What a lot of rot. Never heard such a lot of rot!" But within a fortnight she'd begun to get the hang of it, and it made all the difference to her. She stopped grousing and fussing, and doing things so badly that they worried her. Do nothing.

—RONALD BLYTHE
The View in Winter

*S*he was a high-school principal's widow, now in a home for the elderly, one step short of a nursing home.

She was not unfailingly sweet, gentle, benign. She was at times salty, opinionated, outspoken. But above all she was *fun*. I'll never forget her laughter, great rollicking gusts of sheer joy. I'll never forget either her gift for friendship. People doted on her, adored her.

Still, she had doubts about herself, doubts most of all about her "usefulness." "I can't do anything now," she lamented. "I can't give anything. I'm just putting in time."

"Erva," I replied "it's true you can't do what you once did. But don't you see? You bless the people every day of your life. You bless them just by what you are. I know, every time I visit you I leave a happier person. Erva, what you give is immeasurable."

In seed time learn, in harvest teach, in winter enjoy.

—WILLIAM BLAKE

Charles de Montalembert, the nineteenth-century French Catholic apologist, in his *Monks of the West,* believed that the genuine religious enjoyed benefits

in old age which the more earth-
bound personality could scarcely
imagine. For, besides possessing a
vocation which allowed him special access to the wonder of the
world, life for him "was pro-
longed without being saddened."
The religious, he said, could take
pleasure in and propagate *benignitas*, which he describes as a
purified benevolence. *Benignitas*
was the legitimate last stage of
their religious vocation. They
continued to exist in order to dis-
play *benignitas*; it was their
senescent function. *Benignitas*,
he added, had to take its place
alongside the earlier monastic
virtues of *simplicitas* and *hilari-
tas*, "thus creating the special

fragrance and significance" of the
old man of prayer.

—RONALD BLYTHE
The View in Winter

To grow old is to pass from
passion to compassion.

—ALBERT CAMUS

In these evening years I
cannot equal the accomplish-
ments of earlier times.
I can, however, write a letter,
wash the dishes,
visit a friend;
I can do the shopping,

plant a garden,
   enjoy the view;
I can go for a walk, listen
   to Mozart,
      play with a child.
I can do all the quiet little
things of life in such a way
      as to gladden Your
      heart.

To say that youth is happier than
maturity is like saying that the
view from the bottom of a tower
is better than the view from the
top. As we ascend the spiral stair-
case, and glance from time to
time through the narrow slits in
the stone, the range of our view

widens immensely; the horizon is pushed farther away. Finally as we reach the summit it is as if we had the world at our feet.

—WILLIAM LYON PHELPS

It may well be that there will come a time when I am old and feeble, helpless even. But even then, I hope, there will be one thing I still can do for others: remember them in my prayers.

It would be a perfect ending, spending my latter days in the spirit of love. And who knows? The whispered praise and prayers of an enfeebled old man may prove to be, here and there, a minor means of grace.

When the signs of age begin to mark my body (and still more when they touch my mind); when the ill that is to diminish me or carry me off strikes from without or is born within me; when the painful moment comes in which I suddenly awaken to the fact that I am ill or growing old; and above all at that last moment when I feel I am losing hold of myself and am absolutely passive within the hands of those great unknown forces that have formed me; in all those dark moments, O God, grant that I may understand that it is you (provided only my faith is strong enough) who are painfully parting the fibres of my being in order to penetrate to the very marrow of my substance and bear me away within yourself.

—PIERRE TEILHARD DE CHARDIN
In *The Oxford Book of Prayer*,
George Appleton, editor

Do not go gentle into that good
   night,
Old age should burn and rave at
   close of day;
Rage, rage against the dying of the
   light.

—DYLAN THOMAS
The Collected Poems of Dylan Thomas

No, Dylan.
I am with Saint Francis
when, toward the end,
he murmured,
"Welcome, Sister Death!"

O Lord, support us all the day
long, until the shadows lengthen
and the evening comes, and the
busy world is hushed, and the
fever of life is over, and our work
is done. Then in thy mercy grant
us a safe lodging, and a holy rest,
and peace at the last. Amen.

—*The Book of Common Prayer*